Thank God!

And Live
a More Joyful and Confident Life

Linda Louise Clifton

Murrill Hill Press

Copyright © 2018 Linda Louise Clifton/Murrill Hill Press.
First printing edition 2019

All rights reserved. No part of this publication may be reproduced, distributed, or transmitted in any form or by any means, including photocopying, recording, or other electronic or mechanical methods, without the prior written permission from Linda Louise Clifton/Murrill Hill Press, 1589 Skeet Club Road, Suite 102-190, High Point, NC 27265.

www.lindalclifton.com
author@lindalclifton.com

Book editing and cover art design by ImMEDIAte Solutions/Veronica Lee
www.yourimmediatesolutions.com.

Unless otherwise stated, all Scripture quotations are taken from the New King James Version. Copyright © 1982 by Thomas Nelson, Inc. Used by permission. All rights reserved.

Scriptures marked KJV are taken from the KING JAMES VERSION (KJV): KING JAMES VERSION, public domain.

Scripture quotations marked (ESV) are from The ESV Bible (The Holy Bible, English Standard Version), copyright © 2001 by Crossway, a publishing ministry of Good News Publishers. Used by permission. All rights reserved.

Quotations by Elisabeth Elliot taken from the video teaching series, "Suffering is Not for Nothing," by permission of Ligonier Ministries.

Library of Congress Control Number: 2018911786

ISBN: 978-1-7328156-0-5 (Paper Edition)
ISBN: 978-1-7328156-1-2 (E-Book Edition)

Printed in the United States of America
Murrill Hill Press

TABLE OF CONTENTS

Introduction: Thank God Ahead of Time 1

Chapter 1: Do All Things Without Complaining 11

Chapter 2: Rewards of Thankfulness 27

Chapter 3: Every Good Gift Comes From Above .. 45

Chapter 4: We Can Rely on God's Promises 55

Chapter 5: Waiting on God's Timing 71

Chapter 6: Contentment 81

Chapter 7: Inspiration From the Psalms 95

Closing Words: How Blessed We Are 101

Author's Additions

The Relevance of the Old Testament 105

Choose Life 107

DEDICATION

*To my son Shannon and his wife Magna,
my daughter Camille,
and my three wonderful grandchildren
Providence, Zoë, and Champion*

INTRODUCTION

Thank God Ahead Of Time

One day I got a glimpse of the power of thankfulness that would change my life forever. I am careful to express gratitude to the Lord all the time now. Today I feel freer than I ever felt in my life. I can shake things off now. I can press on with joy and confidence in the Lord like I never was able to do before. I have discovered how quickly hope and peace can be restored to our minds when we shift our focus away from our problems and concerns and focus instead on God and His goodness.

So this is what happened on that memorable day. I had received some very bad news about my car. According to the service man at the dealership, the catalytic converter would have to be replaced. Until that day, I don't think I even knew there was

INTRODUCTION

such a thing as a catalytic converter. The cost? Close to $1000! Suddenly, I felt very sorry for myself.

I already had a whole lot going on in my life. I thought to myself, *the camel's back is finally broken. If only I had done something about it when the engine light first came on, maybe it wouldn't have come to this.* I was a believer and follower of Jesus Christ but my life still seemed disorganized. I was constantly in fear that, at any moment, my life would fall completely apart.

Anyway, I got out of the car, marched straight into the house and straight into my bedroom, slamming every door behind me. I flung myself dramatically across the bed and I began to fret, regret, and boo-hoo. I began to sink lower and lower into the depths of despair. Then, before I knew it, the catalytic converter was no longer the main issue. I began to think about every disappointment in my life and every failure. How would this whole "life thing" turn out anyway? How much more could one person take?

Then suddenly, I came to myself. *Hold up!* I thought to myself. I slammed on the brakes and sat straight up as I recognized how fast I was heading down the road of despair. My life was not that bad! God had blessed my family and me in so many ways.

I recalled 1 Thessalonians 5:18: "*In everything give thanks; for this is the will of God in Christ Jesus for you.*" Not an easy thing to do all the time, but I wasn't even coming close. Instead, there I was, murmuring and complaining against Him like in the old days—the days before I had a relationship with Him. God had surely brought me a long way. He had changed my life for the better in so many ways and shown me so many things that I needed to know. I needed to get a grip!

I considered the sunshine, the rain, clean water and clean air, the food on my table, the pots and pans to prepare the food. I did not always thank God for these blessings. In fact, I had to admit, I took most of them for granted.

INTRODUCTION

I thanked God for allowing me to see a brand new day. When I was a child, I thought church people were just being melodramatic when they would thank and praise God for waking them up to see a brand new day. You see, at the age of nine or ten or so, I took for granted that I would always wake up the next morning. I took many things for granted back then simply because I was a child. But now, as an adult, I understand clearly that our heavenly Father deserves our appreciation when He graciously brings us safely through the night to see a brand new day.

I thanked God for the Lord Jesus who saved me and for His Spirit who directs and comforts me. I thanked God for the comfort of His Word. I thought about the freedoms we still get to enjoy in this country every day, like being able to go to a church and worship God freely. In fact, I thanked God for giving me the desire to even want to thank Him, because He is the One who changes our minds and hearts for the good.

Then, I spoke again to God about my car trouble, but not murmuring and complaining this time. I knew everything was going to be alright. I didn't know exactly how it would all work out but I knew it would.

> Be anxious for nothing, but in everything by prayer and supplication, with thanksgiving, let your requests be made known to God (Philippians 4:6-7).

And what was the outcome with my car issues? The Lord made a way. The fix— $95. Years later, my car was just fine. We can trust the Lord. He cares about us. And He is well able to supply our every need. We have every reason to thank Him ahead of time.

The late missionary and speaker, Elisabeth Elliot, encouraged us to go ahead and thank God even as we wait for our answer to manifest. As she said, *"No matter what is about to happen, you already know the truth, that God is in charge; you are not adrift in a sea of chaos."*

When we have a need, even prior to seeing that need fulfilled, let us go ahead and thank God, just

INTRODUCTION

as Jesus did in the following example as described in John 6:8-13:

> Then Jesus lifted up His eyes, and seeing a great multitude coming toward Him, He said to Philip, "Where shall we buy bread, that these may eat?" But this he said to test him, for He Himself knew what he would do. Philip answered Him, "Two hundred denarii worth of bread is not sufficient for them, that every one of them may have a little." One of His disciples, Andrew, Simon Peter's brother, said to Him, "There is a lad here who has five barley loaves and two small fish, but what are they among so many?" Then Jesus said, "Make the people sit down." Now there was much grass in the place. So the men sat down, in number about five thousand. And Jesus took the loaves, and when He had given thanks He distributed them to the disciples, and the disciples to those sitting down; and likewise of the fish, as much as they wanted. So when they were filled, He said to his disciples, "Gather up the fragments that remain, so that nothing is lost." Therefore, they gathered them up, and filled twelve baskets with the fragments of the five barley loaves which were left over by those who had eaten.

In the incident cited, when thousands of hungry people needed to be fed, Jesus did not pray a long prayer. He simply thanked the Father and proceeded in faith with confidence that God had met their needs. And He certainly did meet their needs, with plenty left over.

Notice later in verse 23, how impressed John must have been that Jesus, in that instance, simply thanked the Father and did not pray a long prayer. In verse 23, John referenced the location *"where they ate bread after the Lord had given thanks."*

Now, I would like to talk about my reasons for writing *Thank God!* I have discovered there is a lot to say and a lot to know about being thankful—both about the power of it and the need for it. I have written this book hoping to help others discover, as I have discovered, that thankfulness is truly a life changing way of thinking. I wrote *Thank God!* also as an expression of my gratitude to God for all the good things I can finally see going on in my life and all around me. He is truly an awesome and faithful God. With this book, I proclaim my intention to go all the way with Him—to trust in the goodness and mercy He continuously makes available to all of us through Jesus Christ our Savior.

If you are a believer whose strength and confidence seem somewhat unsteady at the moment, *Thank God!* is certainly for you. If you are a believer who feels pretty confident in your relationship with the Lord, this book will still likely help your growth and understanding. Even if you do not consider yourself a believer at this time, this book may help you come to this point.

I hope you will take your time and read each chapter carefully. I also hope you will read the scriptures presented and not skip over or skim through any of them. I believe each scripture included is important, helpful, fairly straightforward, and understandable. And remember too, God will help us to understand His Word supernaturally if we really desire understanding.

Thank God! is not a long book but I believe it is a powerful book. I think you will also find this book to be a good choice for a weekly Bible study get-together or book club. For this reason, at the end of each chapter, I have included questions that might inspire further discussion within your group.

So dig in and enjoy!

And whatever you do in word or deed, do all in the name of the Lord Jesus, giving thanks to God the Father through Him.

Colossians 3:17

Chapter 1

DO ALL THINGS WITHOUT COMPLAINING

Do all things without complaining and disputing, that you may become blameless and harmless, children of God without fault in the midst of a crooked and perverse generation, among whom you shine as lights in the world.

Philippians 2:14-15

One thing is for sure: life is not sweet and pretty all the time. Unpleasant circumstances often catch us off guard. We may receive startling news concerning our health or the health of someone we love. We are sometimes betrayed by those we love and who we thought loved us. At times, we may feel all alone. When circumstances seem unbearable, we are tempted to complain. When babies do it, we call it fretting (they don't know any better). When babies grow up, we tell them to stop that whining! For grown people, like you and I, this kind of behavior is neither cute nor tolerable. This kind of behavior displeases God. It is a sign to Him that we do not believe He is willing and able to take care of us. We are instructed to do all things without complaining and to be thankful always.

God has a purpose for everything that He allows to happen in the lives of His children. Do you believe that? According to Romans 8:28, *"All things work together for good to those who love God, to those who are the called according to His purpose."* Therefore, we really have no reason to fear. God is at the wheel always. So we can rejoice and be thankful anyway, even if the flight was cancelled, the loan was denied, the job offer did not come through, or family members prove unfaithful. No matter the difficulty, no matter the loss, God's plans are working. We just need to trust Him.

WHEN ISRAEL COMPLAINED

Moses had delivered the final warning to Pharaoh. Unless Pharaoh released the children of Israel out of slavery, death would come to all the firstborn of Egypt. When Pharaoh refused to release the people, all of Egypt's firstborn, both of man and beast, died that night. Israel did not suffer such a loss, however. The death angel passed over Israel's households so that they were not affected. After witnessing this last demonstration of God's power, Pharaoh was finally convinced. He agreed to let the people go.

Still, despite all the amazing miracles the Lord performed on Israel's behalf, Israel continued to doubt the Lord. And what is worse, they continued to doubt the Lord despite His visible presence as described in the following verse:

> And the LORD went before them by day in a pillar of cloud to lead the way, and by night in a pillar of fire to give them light (Exodus 13:21).

Now, let's take a look at specific instances that illustrate Israel's doubting and complaining attitude as they travelled out of Egypt and on to the Promised Land.

At the Red Sea

After Pharaoh agreed to let Israel go and they had departed for the Promised Land, Pharaoh had a change of heart. He decided he would go after Israel and force them to return to Egypt. In fact, as Israel approached the Red Sea, Pharaoh and his army in over six hundred chariots were right on Israel's heels. With the Red Sea in front of them and Pharaoh and his men right on their heels, Israel murmured and complained to Moses.

> "Because there were no graves in Egypt, have you taken us away to die in the wilderness? Why have you so dealt with us, to bring us up out of Egypt? Is this not the word that we told you in Egypt, saying, 'Let us alone that we may serve the Egyptians'? For it would have been better for us to serve the Egyptians than we should die in the wilderness" (Exodus 14:11-12).

And what did the Lord do?

The Lord parted the Red Sea so that the children of Israel could cross over on dry ground. Then the sea came back upon Pharaoh and his men, and they were drowned in the sea.

They Complained of Hunger

> "Oh, that we had died by the hand of the LORD in the land of Egypt, when we sat by the pots of meat and when we ate bread to the full! For you have brought us out into this wilderness to kill this whole assembly with hunger" (Exodus 16:3).

And what did the Lord do?

The Lord rained down bread from heaven (manna). And when they despised the manna and began to complain because they wanted meat, God sent them quail from the sea.

They Complained of Thirst

> And the people complained against Moses, and said, "Why is it you have brought us up out of Egypt, to kill us and our children and our livestock with thirst?" (Exodus 17:3).

And what did the Lord do?

The Lord commanded Moses to strike the rock with his rod, and when Moses did, water came out of the rock for the people to drink.

They Complained in Moses' Absence

When Moses met with the Lord on Mount Sanai, where the Lord revealed to Moses the Ten Commandments and the other laws of the Lord, the people grew impatient and began to complain.

> The people gathered together to Aaron, and said to him, "Come, make us gods that shall go before us; for as for this Moses, the man who brought us up out of the land of Egypt, we do not know what has become of him" (Exodus 32:1).

When we skip down to verse 4, we discover Aaron the prophet fashioned a molded calf from the gold the people provided him. They worshipped their man-made god and proclaimed he was the one who had brought them out of the land of Egypt.

They Refused to Enter the Promised Land

When Moses sent men to spy out the Promised Land, the men returned with a negative report and the people complained.

> "Why has the LORD brought us to this land to fall by the sword, that our wives and children should become victims? Would it not be better for us to return to Egypt?" So they said to one another, "Let us select a leader and return to Egypt" (Numbers 14:3-4).

And what did the Lord do?

Finally, God pronounced severe judgment upon the grumblers and complainers. They would not be allowed to enter the Promised Land. Of those who were twenty years old or older when they left Egypt, only Joshua and Caleb (because they remained faithful to the Lord) would be allowed to enter the Promised Land. All the others would die in the wilderness.

A very sad story, isn't it? Despite all the miraculous works of the Lord that the Israelites witnessed, Israel still did not trust the Lord. If Israel had trusted Him and believed His word, they would not have kicked and screamed all the way as they did; they would not have found fault with every detail.

When we find ourselves murmuring and complaining about the rain, the heat, the cold, our jobs, our families, our finances, and everything else, let us remember that God is not pleased with this kind of behavior. When we behave this way, we show Him we do not trust Him or appreciate all He does for us. Remember, He put up with Israel's behavior for quite a while, but then, enough was enough.

GIVING THANKS IS NOT AN OPTION

One way to determine if we are in or out of the will of God is to examine how thankful we are towards Him. 1 Thessalonians 5:18 tells us: *"In everything give thanks; for this is the will of God in Christ Jesus for you."* So let us examine ourselves. If we are grumpy, ill-tempered, and constantly complaining most of the time, we surely need to ask God's forgiveness and take steps to correct this kind of ungodly behavior.

In Romans 1 starting with verse 18, the apostle Paul describes the continuous moral decline of those who refused to acknowledge God and thank Him. Although they knew God, they tried to suppress their knowledge of God. But how had they come to know God? According to verse 19, God has placed the knowledge of Himself in the hearts of all men. Not only that, but according to verse 20, His eternal power and divine nature are revealed in everything He has created.

Then, according to verse 21: *"Although they knew God, they did not glorify Him as God, nor were thankful, but became futile in their thoughts, and their foolish hearts were darkened."* When they refused to acknowledge and worship the true and living God, the Creator of all things, they began to worship idol gods. As we have seen, Israel's continued lack of faith and gratitude in the wilderness also led them to practice idolatry. Idol worship would continue be a problem down through the ages, not only for Israel but also for all men. Whatever is valued more than God is valued is an idol, whether family, career, money, possessions, or any other thing.

Finally, in verse 28, we read that God gave over to a debased mind those who refused to acknowledge and thank Him. Then they would take part in all kinds of wicked deeds: sexual immorality, covetousness, maliciousness, envy, murder, strife, evil-mindedness, hatred of God, lack of forgiveness, lack of mercy, and the list goes on.

Thanking God then is not an option. It is a requirement. Refusing to acknowledge and express our appreciation for God can carry grave consequences. We saw this with Israel in the wilderness. It is also true for today.

ONE MAN WHO DID NOT COMPLAIN

Now, let's take a look at an individual who made the most of some very difficult situations and never complained. He was subjected to all kinds of undeserved mistreatment—lies, insults, betrayals, abandonment, and imprisonment. He never gave into discouragement but always maintained his confidence in the goodness of God. In every tough situation he had to deal with, he never complained, and God blessed him in every case. The person I am referring to is Joseph.

Joseph was Jacob's favorite son, and for that very reason, he was greatly resented by his brothers. When Joseph told his brothers about a strange dream he had one night, which seemed to imply he would one day rule over them, they resented him even more (see Genesis 37:5-8). They were all older than Joseph (except Benjamin) so why in the world should they ever have to bow down to him?

Then, Joseph dreamed a second dream, which seemed to imply he would be given a place of authority over not only his brothers but also his father and mother. Even Joseph's father rebuked him: *"Shall your mother and I and your brothers indeed come to bow down to the earth before you?"* (Genesis 37:10).

Joseph's brothers hated Joseph so much that they considered killing him. They decided, instead, to sell him to slave traders. The slave traders then sold Joseph to Potiphar, an officer of the pharaoh of Egypt.

The Bible tells us, in everything Joseph did for Potiphar, he was successful, for the Lord was with Joseph (Genesis 39:2). In fact, Potiphar was so impressed with Joseph, he put Joseph in charge of his entire household and over everything he owned.

Later however, Potiphar would have Joseph thrown into prison because he believed his wife's false accusations against Joseph. But even in prison, the Lord was with Joseph (Genesis 39:21).

Now, during the time Joseph was in prison, Pharaoh began to dream some very disturbing dreams. He heard Joseph was able to interpret dreams, so he called on Joseph. Joseph told Pharaoh that his dreams warned of a seven-year famine in the land. However, there was some good news. Before the famine was to strike, seven years of great plenty would occur.

Joseph urged Pharaoh to appoint someone to set up a system of food storage during the good years in anticipation of the famine. Because Pharaoh was so impressed with Joseph's wisdom and discernment, he appointed Joseph to carry out that important role. In that position, Joseph became second only to Pharaoh in command of the region.

Now, during the famine, Joseph's brothers were among those who traveled to Egypt to purchase food. They did not realize Joseph had anything to do with the reason food was available in Egypt. Glad to see his brothers, Joseph assured them, *"Do not therefore be grieved or angry with yourselves because you sold me here. . . God sent me before you to preserve a posterity for you in the earth, and to save your lives by a great deliverance"* (Genesis 45:5, 7).

Joseph further assured his brothers: *"You meant evil against me; but God meant it for good, in order to bring it about as it is this day, to save many people alive"* (Genesis 50:20). God allowed Joseph to be sold into slavery and brought to Egypt to help save the lives of many people, including the lives of the brothers who had wanted to kill him.

And this is the bottom line for all of God's children. There are blessings in any hardship God allows to happen in the lives of His children. For this reason, we can remain thankful even when confronted with difficult situations we do not understand.

> All things work together for good to those who love God, to those who are the called according to His purpose (Romans 8:28).

God is certainly the great orchestrator, isn't He? He knows what He is doing. In the words of the missionary Elisabeth Elliot, *"No matter what is about to happen, you already know the truth, that God is in charge. You are not adrift in a sea of chaos."*

We don't need to fuss and complain when seemingly negative situations come our way. Thank God He uses everything to bring about good on our behalf. Our circumstances may not feel so good at every moment, but we can be sure that, if God allows it, it is for our good. Time will surely reveal it. If we could see the whole picture, we would know that everything is tying together wonderfully well. So let's be grateful always. There is never any need to complain.

Let's Think/Talk/Write About It

- Why are murmuring and complaining so displeasing to God?

- How would you define the term idol? Describe man's progression to idol worship? In the wilderness, how did Israel get to that point?

- What are the golden calves commonly created and worshipped in today's society?

- How do we guard against idol worship?

- In general, do believers' attitudes and behaviors seem all that different from the attitudes and behaviors of Israel in the wilderness? Discuss.

I will give thanks to the LORD with all my heart; I will recount all of your wonderful deeds.

Psalm 9:1 (ESV)

Chapter 2

REWARDS OF THANKFULNESS

*"Whoever offers praise glorifies Me;
and to him who orders his conduct aright
I will show the salvation of God."*

Psalm 50:23

When we genuinely appreciate the Lord and all He does for us, I believe we are then in the right frame of mind and position to receive everything He has for us. When we take time to meditate on the Lord and to thank Him and praise Him, He is then magnified in our minds and hearts as our worries, fears, doubts, and selfish concerns are all pushed aside. We are empowered then to more easily receive God's blessings.

You may be surprised to learn of the many areas in our lives that are positively affected by a thankful attitude. I certainly was surprised. Let's take a look at some of these.

HEALTH AND WELLNESS

When we are more appreciative, we often begin to feel better and may even begin to look a little better too. Regardless of age, brighter eyes and glowing skin usually result, for example. Compare this to the appearance of a person who is always dissatisfied, always grumpy, always murmuring, and always complaining. The differences are more apparent than we might think.

Gratitude is also good for the heart. As reported on National Public Radio in a program titled "Gratitude Is Good for The Soul and Helps the Heart Too," a long time heart health researcher, Paul Mills, conducted a study involving 186 men and women (average age 66) who had some damage to their hearts. Based on a questionnaire they were asked to complete in order to rate how grateful they felt for the people, places, and things in their lives, it was determined that those who were more grateful were also healthier. Those who were more grateful were less depressed, slept better, had more energy, and experienced less inflammation.

Then Mills conducted a follow-up study with 40 patients. After assessing the heart health of the patients, he asked half of them to regularly write in a journal about two or three things they felt grateful for. After two months, those who kept a gratitude journal experienced a decrease in risk factors for heart disease. Their inflammation levels decreased and their heart rhythms improved. Gratitude is good for the heart, according to Mills, because it helps reduce stress, depression, and anxiety, which are all huge factors for heart disease.

Robert Emmons Ph.D., a leading gratitude researcher, has also discovered a link between gratitude and sleep. As you probably know, lack of adequate sleep affects the heart, the immune system, and also the body's ability to heal. Lack of sleep can also contribute to the presence of diseases such as diabetes, obesity, chronic pain, memory loss, and the ability to concentrate. Emmons discovered that people who spend 15 minutes before bedtime jotting down what they are grateful for tend to fall asleep faster and stay asleep longer.

Researchers are also finding a connection between a person's thoughts and their bone density. Bone density, as you probably know, is a very important health factor affecting our mobility and safety, especially as we age. God's Word said it first: *"A joyful heart is good medicine, but a crushed spirit dries up the bones"* (Proverbs 17:22, ESV). Later in this chapter, we will see more clearly the connection between joy and thankfulness.

A thankful attitude has also been found to help lower a person's blood pressure and help achieve better health outcomes for those undergoing medical procedures such as surgery.

EXCELLENCE AND INCREASE

When we appreciate all that God has provided for us, we will not want to waste or misuse any of our blessings. We will not take for granted the people, things, or opportunities God has placed in our lives. We will take better care of our health by doing the things that promote good health and long life. Thankful students take advantage of their opportunities by staying in school and performing their best while in school. Thankful employees show up to work on time, do a good job, and try to make a difference in their workplaces. Thankful business owners treat their employees and customers well and provide great service. When we appreciate and manage well what we already have, we are in position to receive more from the Lord. Compare this kind of behavior with the arrogant and wasteful behavior of those who have no appreciation for what God has given them.

Thankful people are also nicer to others and easier to be around. Since they realize their value in the eyes of God, they no longer fear and resent others as they might have in the past. People who are thankful do not envy others, compare themselves with others, or compete with others. Thankful people are also less combative.

All of these changes lead to increase. When we appreciate what God has given us, when we give Him the glory for all we have, and when we gladly take care of what we have, we will experience increase in those areas; it cannot turn out any other way. On the other hand, when we do not feel and express gratitude for the resources and advantages we have and do not properly manage our resources, they will likely slip away.

WE CAN GET TO KNOW THE LORD BETTER

Elisabeth Elliot, the well-respected missionary, speaker, and writer, described gratitude as a shortcut to learning to know God. She talked about this in the excellent video teaching series "Suffering Is Not for Nothing," which is available online through Ligonier Ministries.

The bottom line is this: when we look for God, we will find Him. When we begin to pay attention and acknowledge the many ways He demonstrates His love towards us every single day, we will develop a greater awareness of Him and appreciation for Him. Our desire for Him will then grow. We will begin to talk to Him more, listen to Him more, talk about Him more, and desire to study His Word more. And so our progress in the Lord will grow in this way.

Sadly, many of us do not know the Lord very well. Therefore, we are not able to relax and trust Him as we should. This seems to be true even among those of us who profess to follow Him. We can get to know more about the Lord simply by paying closer attention to all He does and has done for us. What are some of these things? He gives us light and sunshine (we need that vitamin D, don't we?), the rain too, a good night's sleep, hot and nourishing meals, smiles and lighthearted laughter, the comfort and joy of our families, enjoyment in doing the things He has gifted us to do, and so many other wonderful blessings that we often take for granted.

We want to get to the place where thoughts of the Lord overwhelm any negative and ungodly thoughts that try to invade our minds. As we grow in this, so also will grow our awareness that He is with us and on our side through Christ Jesus. As our faith and confidence in Him grow, we will see even greater things begin to happen.

JOY

Now, joy is not the same as happiness; let's be clear about that. Happiness usually depends upon one's current circumstances and is therefore a temporary state of mind. For instance, when you get promoted, you feel happy, at least for a while. When you buy a new car, you feel happy, at least until you have to make the first car payment. But if you really believe God, even if you lose your job or wreck your car, you are still able to experience joy in your heart. Why is that? Because you know in your heart that God is working out all things for your good. Joy then does not depend on how much you have, but it depends on how much you appreciate whatever you have.

If we are not thankful we are usually miserable, grumpy, and constantly complaining. Sadly, this is often the go-to response for many of us when we encounter difficulties of any kind. The important point is this: we are responsible for our choices. We can choose either misery or joy.

Many people think they will experience more joy once they achieve a certain status in life. Maybe it's marriage, an exciting career, a home, children, or something else. But real joy does not depend upon a person's circumstances. Joy is actually a gift that the Spirit of God gives to every believer (see Galatians 5:22). However, we must do our part to keep this joy stirred up in our hearts. When our eyes are opened to recognize the abundance of God's blessings, joy is stirred up in our hearts. And as we concentrate on the good things in our lives, those things which are true, honorable, just, pure, lovely, commendable, excellent, and worthy of praise (see Philippians 4:8), joy is stirred up in our hearts.

> "Do not sorrow, for the joy of the LORD is your strength"(Nehemiah 8:10).

The joy of the Lord strengthens us and helps us to move forward in what God has called us to do. Instead of thinking woe-is-me thoughts, we remember God's goodness and the good things He is accomplishing in our lives. We do not allow our minds to be burdened with worries, fear, or despair. We allow the joy of the Lord to renew and refresh us. We are enabled to *"mount up with wings like eagles . . . run and not be weary . . . walk and not faint"* (see Isaiah 40:31).

FREEDOM

Freedom is something we all desire. We like the idea of having the freedom to do the things that mean the most to us. Few of us would look forward to spending years in a 6 x 8 foot prison cell unable to see the people we love or do the things we love to do.

Many different kinds of situations can restrain us or even imprison us, whether mentally, physically, or spiritually. We can be bound by our fearful and anxious thoughts and tormenting memories, for example. But God wants us free. In fact, Jesus came and died to make freedom a reality for all of us.

If we will keep our thoughts on the Lord, acknowledge Him in all we do, and express appreciation for Him at all times, we can enjoy the freedom He desires we enjoy. Let's take a look at a few examples to see how this works.

David Surrounded by His Enemies

In Psalm 18, David described a time when he felt surrounded and confined by his enemies. He described this situation in the following verse:

> The pangs of death surrounded me, and the floods of ungodliness made me afraid. The sorrows of Sheol surrounded me; the snares of death confronted me (verses 4-5).

What did David do?

David cried out to the Lord for deliverance from his enemies. He also praised the Lord and acknowledged the Lord's goodness and power to deliver him. We read his words for example:

> The LORD is my rock and my fortress and my deliverer; my God, my strength, in whom I will trust; my shield and the horn of my salvation, my stronghold (verse 2).

And how did the Lord respond to David's cries?

> [The LORD] sent from above, He took me;
> He drew me out of many waters.
> He delivered me from my strong enemy,
> From those who hated me,
> For they were too strong for me.
> They confronted me in the day of my calamity,
> But the LORD was my support.
> He also brought me out into a broad place;
> He delivered me because He delighted in me (verses 16-19).

The Lord delivered David to a place where he was no longer surrounded by his enemies—a place where there was plenty of room, where he was no longer hemmed in by his enemies. At last, David could breathe freely and move around freely.

Jonah in the Belly of the Whale

Jonah's confinement in the belly of the whale is described in the second chapter of Jonah. Jonah said of his confinement:

> "The waters surrounded me, even to my soul; the deep closed around me; weeds were wrapped around my head" (verse 5).

What did Jonah finally decide to do?

> "I will sacrifice to [the LORD] with the voice of thanksgiving; I will pay what I have vowed. Salvation is of the LORD" (verse 9).

And how did the Lord respond?

> So the LORD spoke to the fish, and it vomited Jonah onto dry land (verse 10).

The Woman with a Spirit of Infirmity

As recorded in Luke 13, one day Jesus was teaching in the synagogue and *"there was a woman who had a spirit of infirmity eighteen years, and was bent over and could in no way raise herself up"* (verse 11). Because of her infirmity, the woman was bound.

What action did the woman with the infirmity take?

Despite her affliction, the woman still made her way to the synagogue. She obviously would have glorified the Lord in the synagogue. Her determination surely made an impression on Jesus, for He took notice of her.

And what did Jesus do?

> He called her to Him and said to her, "Woman, you are loosed from your infirmity." And He laid His hands on her, and immediately she was made straight, and glorified God (verses 12-13).

Paul and Silas in Prison

Now, let's read in Acts 16 concerning Paul and Silas. They were thrown into an actual prison because of their audacity to preach the gospel. We learn that the magistrates tore off the clothes of Paul and Silas and ordered that they be beaten. Then with their feet fastened in the stocks, they were cast into the inner prison.

What did Paul and Silas do?

> And at midnight Paul and Silas prayed, and sang praises unto God: and the prisoners heard them (verse 25, KJV).

Notice what Paul and Silas did not do. They did not tremble in fear nor did they murmur and complain. Even under such harsh circumstances, they praised the Lord.

And what was the outcome?

> Suddenly there was a great earthquake, so that the foundations of the prison were shaken; and immediately all the doors were opened and everyone's chains were loosed (verse 26).

Suddenly and miraculously, the prisoners' chains were loosed and the prison doors opened. As a result of Paul and Silas' expressions of praise and thanksgiving, with the prison doors opened, they certainly could have escaped if they had chosen to do so.

VICTORY IN BATTLE

Do you believe we can thank and praise our way to victory? Let's go to 2 Chronicles 20 where this actually happened.

We read in 2 Chronicles that a coalition of nations had come together to battle against the city of Jerusalem. Once King Jehoshaphat learned of their plans, he called the people together to fast and pray to the Lord concerning the impending threat.

What else did King Jehoshaphat do?

> And when [Jehoshaphat] had consulted with the people, he appointed those who should sing to the LORD, and who should praise the beauty of holiness, as they went out before the army and were saying:
>
> "Praise the LORD,
> For His mercy endures
> forever" (2 Chronicles 20: 21).

As the people of Judah sang praises to the Lord, the threat from their enemies was totally squashed.

And what happened?

> So when Judah came to a place overlooking the wilderness, they looked toward the multitude; and there were their dead bodies, fallen on the earth. No one had escaped (verse 24).

The nations that had assembled together against Judah got confused somehow and began to attack one another. And all of Judah's enemies were killed. Truly amazing!

Can we today experience supernatural victory as Judah did? Yes, I believe it is possible that we can observe our enemies attack and defeat one another without our ever having to lift a finger. We are never without help. As we make our requests to the Lord, let us joyously sing, dance, and praise the Lord, just as Judah did, and let us watch Him work it out.

Let's Think/Talk/Write About It

- Elisabeth Elliot described gratitude as an easy way to get to know God better. Do you agree with this statement? Discuss.

- What is joy in the Lord? How does thankfulness increase joy in our lives?

- Do you believe there is a connection between your thoughts and how you feel physically? Do you agree that a thankful attitude makes a difference? Discuss.

- Can thanking and praising God open prison doors today? Explain. How can thanking and praising God win battles today? What part does joy play in such instances

Chapter 3

EVERY GOOD GIFT COMES FROM ABOVE

Every good gift and every perfect gift is from above, and comes down from the Father of lights.

James 1:17

If we are convinced that every good gift comes from our Heavenly Father, then He is the One we will be careful to thank for all the good things in our lives. We will thank Him and praise Him lavishly for all of our blessings. We will boast in Him and not in ourselves. But if we tend to ignore the Lord as we go about living our lives and making our decisions, then, for whatever success we experience, we will thank ourselves—not the Lord.

We are often very proud of ourselves because of the good things we do: going to work every day, training our children to be well behaved and responsible, taking care of aging parents, giving to charity, refusing to litter, and similar deeds. We may think we do all of these things on our own and because of our own goodness, but God is the One who created us and He is the One who provides us with the knowledge and physical strength to do such things. He is the One who makes all good things possible.

LET'S SAY GRACE

Six or seven of my former co-workers and I used to get together for lunch most days in our company cafeteria. All in our early to mid-thirties, we seemed to share similar values, similar hopes and dreams, and similar concerns for our families and ourselves. All of us attended church regularly, or at least I assumed so.

One day at lunch, my co-worker Cynthia asked if we would like to bow our heads as she said grace. Usually, we prayed individually, but everyone happily agreed with Cynthia's idea except Shirley. Shirley seemed to be raising some kind of objection. "*Well, I personally give myself and my husband thanks for the food I'm about to eat!*" Shirley announced boldly.

Everybody's mouths dropped open in disbelief. *Did I imagine it or did the servers suddenly duck down behind the counters? Did I suddenly see lightening? Did I hear thunder?*

Shirley continued unapologetically: "*We get up every morning and go to work to be able to pay for the food we eat.*" Was she kidding? I looked at her face. I looked at her eyes. Nope, she wasn't kidding.

I was tempted to run. I was afraid lightening was going to come down through the roof and get Shirley for saying such things and maybe even get the rest of us for associating with her. I wondered where she thought she and her husband got the health and strength to go to work, manage their money, and shop for food. Who did she think provided them with the intelligence to successfully perform their jobs?

> What do you have that you did not receive? Now if you did indeed receive it, why do you boast as if you had not received it? (1 Corinthians 4:7).

Shirley and her husband both held professional jobs. They lived in an upscale neighborhood. Everybody in her family was healthy, attractive, and smart. The two teenaged boys played sports in high school and would soon be headed off to college. God had provided her family with such great advantages, but for all of those wonderful advantages, she thanked only her husband and herself.

As you can probably imagine, I never was able to look at Shirley in the same way after that. But as I think about it now, I did not always give God the credit for my blessings either. I was certainly never as outspoken and disrespectful as Shirley, but in too many instances, I either neglected to thank God as He deserved or I took the credit for the good things that happened in my life. The truth is, we may not say it as boldly as Shirley said it, but we often think we are responsible for forging our own way in this world. We therefore think, on some level, that good things occur in our lives because we are just that awesome. Our trust then is in ourselves, not God. This is pride and God does not put up with pride.

PRAISE THE LORD!

Although there are many people in the world who think like Shirley, let us be inspired by those who express gratitude to God for their blessings with beautiful words of thanksgiving and praise. Let's look at a few of these cases from God's Word. In each case, just a portion of the individual's words of thanksgiving and praise is presented. However, I believe you will be truly blessed if you will read each passage in full.

David Praised the Lord

When David was finally delivered out of the hands of King Saul, David praised God with these words:

> It is God who avenges me,
> And subdues the peoples under me,
> He delivers me from my enemies.
> You also lift me up above those who rise against me;
> You have delivered me from the violent man.

> Therefore I will give thanks to You, O LORD,
> among the Gentiles,
> And sing praises to Your name (Psalm 18:47-49).

Daniel Blessed God

When Nebuchadnezzar, the king of Babylon, became disturbed by his dreams, he called upon the wise men of the land, (magicians, astrologers, sorcerers, and the Chaldeans) to uncover the meaning of his dreams. When none of them were able to do so, Nebuchadnezzar sent out the command to destroy all of the wise men of Babylon.

> The decree went out, and they began killing the wise men; and they sought Daniel and his companions, to kill them (Daniel 2:13).

So Daniel and his companions were included in the decree, but why would that be? They were Israelites, after all. They worshipped Jehovah. They certainly were not magicians. We discover the answer in Daniel 1:17, which tells us God gave Daniel *"understanding in all visions and dreams."* So yes, Daniel and his companions possessed knowledge and wisdom in many different areas, but unlike the wise men of the land, their knowledge and wisdom came from God.

Now, when Daniel learned that he and his three friends were about to be slaughtered, he asked the king to give him a little time to uncover his dreams' meaning. Then Daniel and his three friends prayed to God and God revealed the meaning of the king's dreams to Daniel in a night vision.

When God answered Daniel's prayers, Daniel blessed God. Daniel acknowledged it was God who had revealed the meaning of Nebuchadnezzar's dreams. Daniel did not credit himself for such a great outcome.

> "Blessed be the name of God forever and ever.
> For wisdom and might are His....
> He gives wisdom to the wise.
> And knowledge to those
>   who have understanding.
> He reveals deep and secret things;
> He knows what is in the darkness,
> And light dwells with Him.

"I thank You and praise You,
O God of my fathers;
You have given me wisdom and might,
And have now made known
    to me what we asked of You,
For You have made
    Known to us the king's demand"
(Daniel 2:20-23).

Mary Magnified the Lord

And finally, we will look at the words of Mary who felt humbled at the news that God had chosen her to carry and bring into the world the Savior Jesus Christ. Mary might have considered herself special and deserving because God had chosen her to play such an awesome role in His plan, but she did not feel that way. Instead, she felt humble. In her prayer of thanksgiving to God, she expressed her sense of awe that He would bestow such a blessing upon her.

She was not a wealthy or a well-known person. She thought of herself as God's lowly servant. She recognized the truth that God bestows mercy and kindness on those of a lowly condition.

And Mary said:
"My soul magnifies the Lord,
And my spirit has rejoiced in God my Savior.
For He has regarded the lowly state of His maidservant; For behold, henceforth all
    generations will call me blessed.
For He who is mighty has
    done great things for me,
And holy is His name.
And his mercy is on those
    who fear Him
From generation to generation" (Luke 1:46-50).

Like David, Daniel, and Mary, let us also be careful to praise the Lord lavishly for the good and exciting outcomes in our lives. Let us always remember that all good things come from Him. If there is cause for any boasting, then, let our boasting always be in the Lord.

Let's Think/Talk/Write About It

- Can you recall an instance of extraordinary victory in your life? Did you lavishly thank and praise God? Describe what happened.

- What is pride? Why is this an important subject to consider when talking about thankfulness?

- What is an appropriate response when someone makes a very big deal about a good job you performed? What are the issues involved?

- Is it appropriate to express thanks to others? Discuss the issues.

- Take one of the examples of thanks and praise cited here. How does it inspire you to thank and praise God more?

Chapter 4

WE CAN RELY ON GOD'S PROMISES

God is not a man, that He should lie,
Nor a son of man, that He should repent.
Has He said, and will He not do?
Or has He spoken, and will He not make it good?

Numbers 23:19

Concerning God's promises, we can rest assured they will absolutely and always come to pass. So if God has spoken to your heart concerning a matter and promised it will work out well for you, you can certainly count on it. It may not happen immediately, however, as some waiting is often involved. But you can go ahead and start shouting and praising God anyway, for it is surely as good as done.

GOD'S PROMISE TO DAVID

When he was just a teenager, David was anointed king of Israel by the prophet Samuel. There was one small problem though: Israel already had a king named Saul. Even David's brothers and his father Jesse could hardly believe David was chosen from among Jesse's eight sons. Why, from among all of Jesse's sons, would God choose David? After all, David was the youngest and the smallest and he was just a meek shepherd boy. At least, that's how David appeared to the average onlooker. However, God could see David's heart.

Saul, the serving king of Israel, was impressive in stature, strong, and powerful. As king, Saul had deliberately disobeyed God many times. So when God's patience with Saul finally came to an end, He chose David as the next king.

Once Saul realized God's anointing was no longer with him and David had been anointed king, Saul grew increasingly fearful and jealous of David. In fact, Saul made up his mind that he would kill David. So David fled from Saul and he would continue to run from Saul approximately a decade.

DAVID IN THE WILDERNESS

David's escape from Saul brought him into the wilderness. David's wilderness experience would be a difficult but necessary time of testing and preparation for his upcoming role as king. It would be a time when he would learn to draw closer to the Lord and learn to recognize and follow His leading.

Like David, as believers and followers of Jesus, we too can expect to spend some time in the wilderness where we will be tested and equipped to carry out the assignment God has for us. Even Jesus was tested in the wilderness. At the start of Jesus' ministry on earth, according to Matthew 4:1-11, He was led by the Spirit into the wilderness, and for forty days, He was confronted and tested by Satan. In each instance of testing, Jesus responded perfectly with the Word of God. Jesus did not sin. Finally, realizing he had been defeated, Satan gave up and left Jesus.

When David was on the run from Saul, he certainly did not do everything perfectly. He did not always wait on the Lord's instructions and the results were often tragic. For example, when David needed food and supplies, he told Priest Ahimelech that he was out on an important mission for King Saul. Ahimelech knew nothing of the trouble between David and Saul. He thought Saul would have wanted him to help David so he gave David holy bread and the sword that had belonged to the giant Goliath. But when King Saul discovered Ahimelech had helped David, Saul had Ahimelech killed, along with all the other priests (a total of eighty-five) and all of their families.

David made another questionable decision when he chose to hide out in the land of the Philistines. King Achish permitted David and his men to reside in the city of Ziklag. This was a strange arrangement since the Philistines and Israel were long standing enemies. Soon, this living arrangement would prove even more awkward for David and his men. The Philistines were planning to go to war against Israel. King Achish made it known to David that he expected David and his men to fight on their side against Israel.

Would David, the anointed king of Israel, join the Philistine army and fight against his own people? Apparently so. Miraculously though, they were saved from having to fight in the war because the other Philistine rulers did not trust them. Surely, it was God who arranged for their release out of such an awkward dilemma.

Yes, David acted out of desperation at times, but he still loved the Lord and desired to honor and glorify Him. On at least two occasions, David was in a position where he could easily have killed King Saul. But David refused to commit such an act *"against the LORD's anointed."* He believed the Lord would handle Saul's removal in His own way and in His own time. He felt confident that Saul's time would soon come to an end. In this matter, David waited on the Lord as he should have.

DAVID ENCOURAGED HIMSELF

Now, when David and his men were released from the duty of having to fight against Israel, they returned to Ziklag. Upon their return, they discovered that the Amalekites had burned down their city and carried away their wives, their children, and all of their possessions. To make matters even worse for David, his men turned against him and wanted to kill him. David was in deep despair. Surely David felt he had no friend to encourage him, no friend to help strengthen his heart. He knew he had to take steps to reverse his outlook.

So what did he do?

> David encouraged himself in the LORD His God (1 Samuel 30:6, KJV).

But how did David go about encouraging himself in the Lord? We must remember that David wrote many of the psalms—awesome songs of thanksgiving, praise, and worship while he was on the run from Saul. Expressing to God what was on his heart in this way surely helped to strengthen

WE CAN RELY ON GOD'S PROMISES

David's weary soul as it helped to shift his focus from himself and his trials to the power and faithfulness of God.

Psalm 59 is an example that might illustrate how David encouraged himself. In fact, this psalm was written by David while he was on the run from Saul.

Notice, David began by crying out to the Lord for deliverance from his enemies.

> Deliver me from my enemies, O my God;
> Defend me from those who rise up against me.
> Deliver me from the workers of iniquity,
> And save me from bloodthirsty men (verses 1-2).

David's confidence in the Lord's ability to deliver him began to rise up.

> But You, O Lord, shall laugh at them;
> You shall have all the nations in derision.
> I will wait for You, O You his Strength;
> For God is my defense.
> My God of mercy shall come to meet me;
> God shall let me see my desire on my enemies (verses 8-10).

Then, strengthened in the Lord, David began to praise the Lord because of the Lord's mercy and power. And David was strengthened even more.

> I will sing of Your power;
> Yes, I will sing aloud of Your mercy in the morning;
> For You have been my defense
> And refuge in the day of my trouble.
> To You, O my Strength, I will sing praises;
> For God is my defense,
> My God of mercy (verses 16-17).

These are not merely lighthearted phrases to say; these are powerful expressions inspired by the Holy Spirit. As David thought about the goodness of the Lord and put these Spirit inspired thoughts into writing, he was strengthened in his spirit, in his mind, and even in his physical body.

So how did things turn out for David? Concerning the Amalekites, we read further in 1 Samuel 30:8: *"David inquired of the LORD, saying, 'Shall I pursue this troop? Shall I overtake them?' And He answered him, 'Pursue, for you shall surely overtake them and without fail recover all.'"* David did as the Lord instructed him to do and everyone and everything that the Amalekites had taken from them were recovered.

There is power in praising God and waiting on His instructions. Like David, we too can encourage ourselves in the Lord during the difficult times in our lives. We do this when we continue to thank God for all he has done, continue to praise Him for all He is, and continue to maintain our confidence in His ability to rescue us.

AND GOD KEPT HIS PROMISE TO DAVID

God kept his promise to David that he would be crowned king of Israel. When the time was right, when the path was clear, and when David was adequately equipped for the role, he was crowned king, just as God had promised.

God also made another very important promise to David: *"And your house and your kingdom shall be established forever before you. Your throne shall be established forever"* (2 Samuel 7:16). But what did this promise mean exactly? How could David's kingdom continue forever?

God's promise to David of an everlasting kingdom refers to the coming reign of Jesus *"upon the throne of David."* This was further confirmed by the angel who spoke to Mary regarding Jesus, the Son she would bring forth: *"And the Lord God will give Him the throne of His father David. And He will reign over the house of Jacob forever, and of His kingdom there will be no end"* (Luke 1:32-33). How faithful is our God!

When we find ourselves growing impatient and fearful that God has forgotten us, let us not forget the importance of timing. There is an appropriate time for all things, and only God knows what that appropriate time is. Only He knows when conditions are just right for the fulfillment of His promise. Only He knows when our hearts are right and able to receive the promise.

GOD'S PROMISES FOR US TODAY

We as believers and followers of Jesus Christ also have many wonderful promises of God that we can believe and hold onto. We can absolutely rely on these promises, for we are told in 2 Corinthians 1:20 that *"all the promises of God in [Jesus Christ] are Yes, and in Him Amen, to the glory of God through us."* So let us not grow weary or impatient if we must wait a little while before God's promise is fulfilled. Let us continue to rejoice and be thankful, confident in the knowledge that all of His promises will surely come to pass at just the right time.

Here is just a small sample of the many wonderful promises of God we can hold onto with confidence. Refer to this list often and add others from God's Word.

Salvation

> If you confess with your mouth the Lord Jesus and believe in your heart that God has raised Him from the dead, you will be saved (Romans 10:9).

Forgiveness of Sins

> If we confess our sins, He is faithful and just to forgive us our sins and to cleanse us from all unrighteousness (1 John 1:9).

Rest for Our Souls

"Come to Me, all you who labor and are heavy laden, and I will give you rest. Take My yoke upon you and learn from Me, for I am gentle and lowly in heart, and you will find rest for your souls. For My yoke is easy and My burden is light" (Matthew 11:28-30).

Strength

Those who wait on the LORD
Shall renew their strength;
They shall mount up with wings like eagles,
They shall run and not be weary,
They shall walk and not faint (Isaiah 40:31).

Safety

"Whoever listens to me will dwell safely,
And will be secure, without fear of evil"
(Proverbs 1:33).

Health

Do not be wise in your own eyes;
Fear the LORD and depart from evil.
It will be health to your flesh,

And strength to your bones (Proverbs 3:7-8).

Fruitfulness

Blessed is the man
Who walks not in the counsel of the ungodly,
Nor stands in the path of sinners,
Nor sits in the seat of the scornful;
But his delight is in the law of the LORD,
And in His law he meditates day and night.
He shall be like a tree
Planted by the rivers of water,
That brings forth its fruit in its season,
Whose leaf also shall not wither;
And whatever he does shall prosper
(Psalm 1:1-3).

Answers to Our Prayers

"Ask, and it will be given to you; seek, and you will find; knock, and it will be opened to you. For everyone who asks receives, and he who seeks finds, and to him who knocks it will be opened" (Matthew 7:7-8).

Jesus Will Return for His People

"In My Father's house are many mansions; if it were not so, I would have told you. I go to prepare a place for you. And if I go and prepare a place for you, I will come again and receive you to Myself; that where I am, there you may be also" (John 14:2-3).

A New Heaven and a New Earth

"And God will wipe away every tear from their eyes; there shall be no more death, nor sorrow, nor crying. There shall be no more pain, for the former things have passed away" (Revelations 21:4).

Let's Think/Talk/Write About It

- God promised David that David's throne would last forever (see 2 Samuel 7:16). What does this promise mean?

- *"Not a word failed of any good thing which the LORD has spoken to the house of Israel. All came to pass"* (Joshua 21:45). Do you know what this is referring to? Discuss.

- What promise(s) in God's Word have been especially important to you?

Let us hold fast the confession of our hope without wavering, for He who promised is faithful.

Hebrews 10:23

Chapter 5

WAITING ON GOD'S TIMING

And let us not grow weary while doing good, for in due season we shall reap if we do not lose heart.

Galatians 6:9

When we were children and our parents promised we were going someplace like Disneyworld on vacation, I remember how excited we would be. We would want to leave right away. Our parents knew taking off for Disneyworld without planning the trip would be a mistake though. Many arrangements would have to be made first. Money would have to be set aside, reservations made, the car serviced, and the best driving route determined. Our parents knew that all of these things and more would have to be handled ahead of time in order to ensure a smooth, safe, and fun vacation. We were anxious to go, but our parents knew they would be making a big mistake if they were moved by our whining.

Our heavenly Father, whose wisdom goes beyond that of any man, knows the appropriate time for all things. When God makes a promise, we can be sure His promise will come to pass—but only when the time is right. Therefore, we can relax and trust Him.

Sometimes, we are just going to have to wait awhile for our answer to come. Some things happen pretty quickly, but not most things. Maybe even now, you feel you have been waiting a long time for God to come through on your behalf. Maybe you are facing a financial crisis, a family breakup, health issues, or some other difficulty. Maybe you feel God has forgotten all about you.

WHEN DAVID HAD TO WAIT

In the life of David, there came a time when he

also wondered if God had forgotten him. In Psalm 13, he expressed these concerns.

> How long, O LORD? Will You forget me forever?
> How long will You hide Your face from me?
> How long shall I take counsel in my soul,
> Having sorrow in my heart daily?
> How long will my enemy be exalted over me?
> (Psalm 13:1-2).

David expressed his frustration and doubt. He wondered, just as we all do at times, if God had forgotten him. We must be careful that we do not lose our correct perspective or lose our joy. We need to remain confident and courageous, no matter what. But then, David remembered that the Lord was still worthy of praise and honor, no matter what. He began to rejoice in the Lord and praise Him. Despite overwhelming feelings of despair, he recalled how the Lord had come to his rescue in the past. Psalm 13 continues and ends on a high note of rejoicing. Surely, David was encouraged at this point.

> But I have trusted in Your mercy;
> My heart shall rejoice in Your salvation.

> I will sing to the LORD,
> Because He has dealt
> > bountifully with me (Psalm 13:5-6).

God has not forgotten you. Neither has He forgotten me. He is always about the business of accomplishing good things in and for the lives of His children. Yes, we usually want what we want and want it when we want it, but we can relax and be glad and thankful that our Father knows when the time is right for all things. As we get to know Him better, we are better able to remain hopeful, thankful, and even joyful during the waiting seasons of our lives.

In the previous chapter, we saw David was finally crowned king of Israel. This happened only after he was adequately prepared to assume the role and King Saul was dead. David surely needed strengthening in certain areas. His faith would have to be tested, his leadership skills developed, and his ability to persevere strengthened. He would also need to know, without a doubt, the importance of always waiting on the Lord. Only God knows when all is ready.

THE VISION IS FOR AN APPOINTED TIME

Proper timing is everything. We have no reason to fear, no reason to fuss. Our God will accomplish all things when the time is right. He is truly faithful.

We will look now at the prophet Habakkuk and see how he came to understand he could always rely on the Lord's timing. Habakkuk was disturbed by the wicked and violent behavior of the Lord's people, Judah. He questioned the Lord: why did He continue to put up with such wicked and violent behavior from His people? Habakkuk cried out to the Lord because he wanted to know what the Lord intended to do to correct their behavior.

The Lord finally answered Habakkuk. The Lord revealed to Habakkuk that He had a plan already in the works to bring about correction to His people. He was raising up a dreadful, fierce, and violent people, the Chaldeans, whom He would use to punish Judah.

Habakkuk did not care much for that particular plan. Yes, the people needed correction, but why would God allow His people to be utterly destroyed by such a wicked people as the Chaldeans?

The Lord then revealed to Habakkuk that His plan was a three-part plan. After the Chaldeans had punished Judah, they would then be defeated by another nation. Judah would then be delivered.

"The vision is yet for an appointed time," God said to Habakkuk (Habakkuk 2:3). Habakkuk was to write this vision and make it plain on tablets. This would serve as a reminder and a comfort to God's people while they were held in captivity by the Chaldeans. All of these events would come to pass at the time God had appointed.

When Habakkuk came to the understanding that the Lord is always in control and He appoints the times and seasons for all things, Habakkuk's faith grew. He wrote the following beautiful and treasured words, which expressed his confidence and joy in the Lord and his appreciation for Him, no matter the outcome.

> Though the fig tree may not blossom,

Nor fruit be on the vines;
Though the labor of the olive may fail,
And the fields yield no food;
Though the flock may be cut off from the fold,
And there be no herd in the stalls
Yet I will rejoice in the LORD,
I will joy in the God of my salvation
(Habakkuk 3:17-18).

THE FULLNESS OF THE TIME HAD COME

Jesus arrived on earth at just the right time. For thousands of years His arrival had been prophesied by those who hoped they would live to see that day; but of course, they did not.

Do you ever wonder why Jesus came at the time He came? Why not a whole lot sooner? *"When the fullness of the time had come, God sent forth His Son"* (Galatians 4:4). That's the answer. When everything was in place, Jesus came. But what kinds of things might this verse be referring to? Here are a few suggestions.

Under the rule of the Roman Empire, certain world conditions were present that would facilitate the preaching of the Gospel message Jesus delivered. A climate of relative calmness existed at that time. People were allowed to worship as they pleased as long as they caused no trouble. The Jews were allowed to worship in Jerusalem according to their beliefs and customs. In this relatively calm atmosphere, Jesus delivered the Gospel to the Jewish people with little interference from the Roman government.

Later, Paul and other missionaries were able to carry the Gospel of Jesus safely to all the world. The Roman roads made travel easier for Paul and other missionaries. Ships also provided an important means of travel. The advanced postal service of the Roman Empire made it possible for Paul's letters to get to the churches more easily. The shared Greek language facilitated the carrying of the Gospel to all regions.

One day, Jesus will return to set up His earthly reign as King. And when will that occur? When the time is perfectly right and all the prophecies concerning His return have been fulfilled. In fact, it is very possible that we are living right now in the time of His return. This may very well be that season of which the Bible speaks.

SO LET US NEVER GIVE UP!

God fulfills all promises, without exception, but only at the proper time. He knows the right times and seasons for all things. We should be glad about that. Let us never murmur and complain. He works all things out wonderfully well.

> Let us not grow weary while doing good, for in due season we shall reap if we do not lose heart (Galatians 6:9).

Just as David expressed in Psalm 31:14-15, we also can say, *"But as for me, I trust in You, O LORD; I say, 'You are my God.' My times are in Your hand."* We can be glad and thankful because God is faithful. So, no matter what it looks like to us, we can keep rejoicing and acknowledging the goodness of God, knowing that the timing of all events are ultimately in His hands.

Let's Think/Talk/Write About It

- What are some of the reasons we might be called to wait?

- In your impatience, have you ever forced a change, while you suspected all along that the time was not quite right? How did this situation turn out for you? How would you handle things differently if given the opportunity today?

- What productive things might we do during the waiting seasons of our lives?

Chapter 6

CONTENTMENT

Not that I speak in regard to need, for I have learned in whatever state I am, to be content.

Philippians 4:11

So many of us believe we will feel glad, thankful, and even content as soon as we achieve a certain goal or status in life. The goal might be the perfect job, the wedding ring, the baby, the house in the right neighborhood, or some special honor or recognition. But contentment really does not work that way. Contentment is a choice; we can choose contentment at any time. We can decide at this very moment to yield to and be glad about God's will for our lives. Only then will we begin to experience contentment.

Of course, choosing contentment does not mean we are to simply resign ourselves to every sort of circumstance that happens to come our way. We are not to simply sigh and say, "*Oh well*" all the time. No, that's not contentment. That's called complacency—laziness even. We certainly are to take steps to improve our conditions as God opens the doors and provides the opportunities. But in some instances, we just don't know what steps to take; we are not sure what God would want us to do. Then, we are to hold our peace and remain content in the knowledge that no experience is ever random or without purpose in God's economy. We can be sure He is working something out for our good.

Following are several helpful ideas to consider, for those of us who are serious about maintaining a thankful and contented frame of mind.

VARIETY IS GOD'S IDEA

Each of us is a one-of-a-kind designer original. Do you ever think about yourself like that? God created each one of us with a unique set of physical features, personality traits, talents, and abilities. He also chose our parents and chose where we would grow up; we certainly had nothing to do with it. He put each one of us here for a specific purpose. Can you get excited about that? Can you feel glad about your life? Can you feel glad about your journey?

We are all different and that's a very good thing. We come in different sizes and shapes. Think about it: of all the billions of people who have lived on this earth, not one has ever had a fingerprint identical to yours. Isn't that amazing? Each one of us is uniquely equipped to serve others in a particular way. We come with different likes and dislikes and different talents and abilities.

We are blessed to have all kinds of people around us who are able to do all kinds of things that we may not know how to do or even want to do: teachers, farmers, auto mechanics, surgeons, trumpet players, piano tuners, furniture designers, leaders of companies, leaders of countries. So why should we waste our time eyeing with envy what others have? Instead, let's be glad about what others can do; let's be glad about what we can do also. We are all equipped in some way for service.

And whether single or married, with children or without children, whether working or retired, whether young or old, we can and should experience a certain sense of confidence and joy in our current situation and season in life. Each stage of life provides certain opportunities and advantages. Let's be glad in this season and make the most of this time and all times. When we accept and are thankful for who we are and where we are at this moment, we will not covet what others have or what God is doing in the lives of others. We will not have the time to do that if we are busy and excited about the wonderful things God is doing in our own lives.

Variety in the Church Body

In 1 Corinthians 12, the Apostle Paul compares the church body to the physical body. Just as the physical body has many members—eyes, ears, fingers, toes, skin, kidneys, and hundreds of other parts—the church body also has many members. Each member of the physical body and the church body performs a necessary function for the good of the entire body.

> If the whole body were an eye, where would be the hearing? If the whole were hearing, where would be the smelling? (1 Corinthians 12:17).

As in an orchestra, every member of the church body has a specific part to play. According to 1 Corinthians 12:8-10, spiritual gifts among the members of the church body include the word of wisdom, the word of knowledge, faith, gifts of healings, the working of miracles, prophecy, discerning of spirits, different kinds of tongues, and the interpretation of tongues. The Holy Spirit has equipped each member of the church body with at least one spiritual gift for the good of the entire body.

So let's begin to appreciate—even celebrate—our unique qualities. Even more importantly, let's appreciate and celebrate the God who so thoughtfully equipped each of us for service to the whole church body. See how we all benefit from God's love of variety?

"But Lord, What About This Man?"

Jesus' inner circle consisted of twelve disciples whom Jesus recognized as having unique personalities and unique mixes of strengths and weaknesses. When jealousy among His disciples surfaced, Jesus would respond quickly. Let's look at one such instance. Jesus was speaking to Peter about how Peter's death would come.

> "When you were younger, you girded yourself and walked where you wished; but when you are old, you will stretch out your hands, and another will gird you and carry you where you do not wish." This He spoke, signifying by what death he would glorify God. And when He had spoken this, He said to him, "Follow Me" (John 21:18-19).

Jesus' words indicated Peter would suffer crucifixion for the sake of the Gospel. In his youth, Peter would have enjoyed the freedom to go and come as young people do. But in his old age, Peter would be bound and carried away. He would stretch out his hands, which signified he would be nailed to a cross.

How did Peter respond? When Peter turned around and saw *"the disciple whom Jesus loved"* (John apparently), Peter questioned Jesus, *"But Lord, what about this man?"* (verse 21).

Jesus considered Peter's question out of line. He said to Peter: *"If I will that he remain till I come, what is that to you? You follow Me"* (verse 22). Maybe Jesus detected Peter was a little resentful of His relationship with John. Maybe Peter was concerned that John would be treated better than he. But Jesus rebuked Peter for asking such a question. *"What is that to you?"* Jesus asked Peter. Then He added, *"You Follow Me."* In other words, Peter did not need to compare his life or his situation to that of John or anyone else. Everyone's path is unique. Jesus is the only standard by which a person's life should be measured. Only Jesus is worthy of such attention. *"You follow Me"* is Jesus' command to all.

GOD'S PLAN FOR SUCCESS

God had an awesome purpose for Adam and Eve. They were to *"be fruitful and multiply; fill the earth and subdue it; have dominion over the fish of the sea, over the birds of the air, and over every living thing that moves on the earth"* (Genesis 1:28). Seems like quite an impressive and fulfilling job description, doesn't it? You would think so, but it wasn't enough for Adam and Eve.

Adam and Eve wanted it all. If they had believed and appreciated the awesome plan God had laid out for them, this world would not be in the awful mess it is in today. We would never get headaches. We would not have to endure unfair treatment in the workplace or any other place. Children would not be subject to online bullying. Lying, theft, and murder would not exist.

Everything in the garden was available for Adam and Eve's use and enjoyment except for just one tree—the Tree of Knowledge of Good and Evil. But Satan sneaked around Eve and convinced her she could have it all if she wanted it. In fact, Satan told her if she ate the forbidden fruit, she would be just like God. Satan wanted Eve to believe God was selfishly trying to hold out on her and Adam.

So Eve bought Satan's lies and ate the forbidden fruit. Then she gave the fruit to Adam and he also ate of it. They wanted access to everything without restrictions. They wanted to be just like God—to know it all and be able to do it all. Adam and Eve's behavior reflected greed and covetousness. Their behavior reflected a lack of appreciation for all God had given them. And because of their actions, they were banished from the Garden and all of God's creation would be negatively affected.

When we are motivated by greed and covetousness, the most significant aspects of our lives usually suffer. When we strive to get more and more, marriages fail, other important relationships fall apart, our children lose their way, and other adverse outcomes result. Most importantly, our relationship with the Lord suffers. These things happen when we do not adequately appreciate God's provisions and plans for our lives.

God has promised to exalt us if we will honor Him and honor His plan for our lives above our own wants and desires. He always knows best. We can see how this works when we look at the life of Jesus.

> [Jesus] humbled Himself and became obedient to the point of death, even the death of the cross. Therefore God also has highly exalted Him and given Him the name which is above every name. (Philippians 2:8-9).

What are we to do then? We are to use our physical capabilities, our gifts and talents, and even our personal preferences for the accomplishment of God's will in this life. We are not to seek to fulfill our own selfish desires, but we are to seek to do God's will. This is how we experience true success, peace, and contentment.

LET'S KEEP OUR PRIORITIES STRAIGHT

"Whatever you do, do all to the glory of God" is our instruction according to 1 Corinthians 10:31. This should be the bottom line consideration whenever we embark on a particular course of action. This should always be our motivation. Let's explore this idea a little further

CONTENTMENT

Let's go to Luke 10:38-42 where we find Martha preparing a meal for Jesus and His disciples who happen to be guests in her home. Martha is very concerned as she is about the business of preparing the meal. Of course, she wants everything to go well, as would anyone in her situation. Only the best would do for such an honored guest as Jesus.

Martha's sister, Mary, however, does not seem to share Martha's concerns at all. In fact, Mary seems oblivious to what is going on with Martha. She does not even notice that Martha needs her help. What is Mary doing? She is sitting happily and contentedly at Jesus' feet, basking in His presence and hanging onto His every word.

To Martha, Mary's behavior seems irresponsible. Doesn't Mary care that she is needed in the kitchen? Finally, when Martha could stand it no longer, she protests directly to Jesus: *"Lord, do you not care that my sister has left me to serve alone? Therefore tell her to help me"* (verse 40). We surely can relate to Martha's dilemma. After all, Jesus should always be treated like a very special guest!

Does Jesus rebuke Mary for not helping her sister? No, He does not. Jesus responds instead, *"Martha, Martha, you are worried and troubled about many things. But one thing is needed, and Mary has chosen that good part, which will not be taken away from her"* (verses 41-42). What are we to make of Jesus' remark? Seems somewhat unfair, doesn't it?

Martha was certainly performing a necessary and commendable service as she prepared a meal for her guests. But could it be that Martha's motives were not as pure as they could have been? Out of a sense of pride, was she overly concerned about the impression she was making on her guests? Could she have chosen a simpler meal to prepare so that she might have had more time to spend with the Lord? Yes, we are certainly all called to serve and make excellent use of our God-given gifts and talents. But praising and worshipping the Lord and spending time with Him should always be our primary consideration.

What then is contentment? Bottom line, contentment is satisfaction with God. Contentment is trusting God and trusting His plans for us. He created us, after all, and He knows all about us. Only God knows what will bring us real peace, real joy, and real fulfillment.

Let's Think/Talk/Write About It

- Why does envy destroy any chance for contentment? What is the harm in comparing ourselves to others? How can we avoid these behaviors?

- Why are our differences a good thing?

- Would you have been more of a Mary or a Martha in the situation described in Luke 10:38-42? Why do you think so?

- As in Apostle Paul's thorn in the flesh situation, (read 2 Corinthians 12:7-10), gratitude and contentment often require the acceptance of a current situation and/or a past event that we may not fully understand. Why did the Lord not take away Paul's thorn in the flesh? Why was Paul able to remain content in this situation?

Chapter 7

INSPIRATION FROM THE PSALMS

Bless the LORD, O my soul, and forget not all His benefits.

Psalm 103:2

The book of Psalms is filled with beautiful words of praise and appreciation for all that the Lord does and has done. The Psalms is one of two Old Testament books that is most quoted in the New Testament (the other is Isaiah). This indicates the enduring relevance of the Psalms.

Today, the Psalms continue to remind us to express our appreciation to God for the specific acts He does and has done, and to also praise Him because of who He is. He is merciful. He is all-powerful. He is faithful. He sees all. He knows all. He is true. He is love.

The psalmists wrote many of the psalms during times of deep sorrow and disappointment. Still, they expressed confidence in God's goodness, His willingness, and His power to help and deliver His people. The psalms remind us that God is always with us and always on our side, no matter what our circumstances may look like at the moment. They inspire us to trust God and to thank and praise Him at all times.

Excerpts from just a few of these wonderful psalms follow. Hopefully, you will be moved to find them in the Bible and read them in their entirety. In fact, I believe you will be greatly blessed if you will set aside time each day to explore the Book of Psalms. Your understanding and appreciation for the awesome God we serve will surely increase.

Psalm 103 is a good place to start. This psalm encourages us to bless the Lord wholeheartedly for all of His many benefits. Read about His awesome benefits.

Bless the LORD, O my soul;
And all that is within me, bless His holy name!
Bless the LORD, O my soul,
And forget not all His benefits:
Who forgives all your iniquities,
Who heals all your diseases,
Who redeems your life from destruction,
Who crowns you with lovingkindness
    and tender mercies,
Who satisfies your mouth with good things,
So that your youth is renewed like the eagle's
(Psalm 103:1-5).

Psalm 121 reminds us that the Lord is our Help. He will keep our foot from slipping as we go. He will protect us from all harm in our going out and in our coming in.

He will not allow your foot to be moved;
He who keeps you will not slumber.
Behold, He who keeps Israel
Shall neither slumber nor sleep.
The LORD is your keeper;
The LORD is your shade at your right hand.
The sun shall not strike you by day,
Nor the moon by night (Psalm 121:3-6).

Psalm 77 reminds us that recounting the wondrous works of the Lord in days gone by dispels our doubts and fears and restores our confidence in the Lord's power.

> I will remember the works of the LORD;
> Surely I will remember Your wonders of old.
> I will also meditate on all Your work,
> And talk of Your deeds.
> Your way, O God, is in the sanctuary;
> Who is so great a God as our God?
> You are the God who does wonders;
> You have declared Your strength among the peoples (Psalm 77:11-14).

Psalm 100 expresses the importance of thanking and praising the Lord with joy and gladness.

> Make a joyful shout to the LORD, all you lands!
> Serve the LORD with gladness;
> Come before His presence with singing.
> Know that the LORD, He is God;
> It is He who has made us, and not we ourselves;
> We are His people and the sheep of His pasture.
> Enter into His gates with thanksgiving,
> And into His courts with praise.

Be thankful to Him, and bless His name
For the LORD is good;
His mercy is everlasting,
And His truth endures to all
generations (Psalm 100:1-5).

And **Psalm 150**, which is the last psalm, encourages us to praise the Lord with joy and gladness and with instruments and dance.

Praise the LORD!
Praise God in His sanctuary;
Praise Him in His mighty firmament!
Praise Him for His mighty acts;
Praise Him according to His excellent greatness!
Praise Him with the sound of the trumpet;
Praise Him with the lute and harp!
Praise Him with the timbrel and dance;
Praise Him with stringed instruments and flutes!
Praise Him with loud cymbals;
Praise Him with clashing cymbals!
Let everything that has breath praise the LORD
Praise the LORD! (Psalm 150:1-6).

Let's Think/Talk/Write about It

- Which of the psalms of praise quoted in this chapter do you find especially inspiring and helpful at this moment in your life and as you desire to thank and praise the Lord?

- Are there other psalms of praise (not quoted in this chapter) that you find especially inspiring and descriptive of God's goodness?

CLOSING WORDS

How Blessed We Are

A thankful attitude towards God can quickly transport us from despair to joy, peace, and confidence in the Lord. Our minds are blessed and our physical bodies are blessed when we reflect more on what we have and less on what we do not have. Either list will always be infinitely long. No matter what is going on in our lives, let us continue to see ourselves as blessed, as provided for, and cared for. Let us be content.

God has done great things for us. He saved us and delivered us through the death and resurrection of His Son Christ Jesus. We are not defeated. We are not forsaken. We have a lot right here and right now, and the future for us is even brighter.

No matter what is going on in our lives and in the world, we can hold onto our confidence and our thankful attitude, knowing our heavenly Father is in control of all things. His plan is unfolding properly and it is a good plan. In fact, He is a good God. We can thank God because we can depend on Him, no matter how things may look for a season. He is faithful to perform His word. Jesus said, *"Heaven and earth will pass away, but my words will by no means pass away"* (Matthew 24:35). His word will stand forever.

So let us acknowledge God's goodness at all times—whether times seem good or they seem not so good. The Word of God assures us that He is working all things out on our behalf, and bringing about His eternal promises in our lives.

And now I would like to express my thanks to you for taking the time to discover some of the wonderful concepts God has opened up to me regarding this important topic of thankfulness. I hope your life has been positively influenced by all you have read here.

May God bless you.

AUTHOR'S ADDITIONS

The Relevance Of The Old Testament

Some people question the relevance of the Old Testament to our lives today. It is true that today we as believers enjoy direct access to God the Father through Jesus Christ—a great advantage that the Old Testament saints hoped to see. The Old Testament saints understood that Christ's coming would bring about a better day. They prophesied of that day but they did not get to see it. Today, through faith in Jesus Christ alone, we can be forgiven of our sins forever and receive all the blessings that accompany that forgiveness. The sacrifice of bulls and goats as described in the Old Testament was only a temporary fix for forgiveness of sins and had to be performed annually. But today, faith in Jesus Christ—the perfect sacrificial Lamb—is the way of forgiveness for once and for all.

So we thank God for the excellent covenant we enjoy with the Lord today. Still, we have His Word that "all Scripture is given by inspiration of God, and is profitable for doctrine, for reproof, for correction, for instruction in righteousness" (2 Timothy 3:16). This tells me that all of God's dealings with mankind throughout the ages (not just some of them) are relevant to our understanding today. God's principles have not changed; the truth has not changed. Therefore, I am sure you will find helpful all of the examples included here, from the Old Testament and the New.

Choose Life

God allows us to choose our course in this life. We can choose to walk with Him, which leads to life—eternal life, or we can choose to walk contrary to His plan, which leads to death. We get to choose.

> The gift of God is eternal life in Christ Jesus our Lord (Romans 6:23).

Jesus says in John 14:6, *"No one comes to the Father except through Me."* Therefore, if we desire to walk with God, we can only get to Him by way of Jesus. In the same verse, Jesus also states: *"I am the way, the truth, and the life."* So then, life is in Jesus. We cannot receive life and all the benefits of life except through Jesus.

But what does all of this mean really? How do we choose life? I offer the following explanation, which I hope and believe is helpful. I hope also that those who have not done so already will be inspired to take the appropriate steps and choose life.

Back to the Beginning

In the beginning, when Adam and Eve were the only human beings who walked the earth, life was perfect; sin did not exist. Adam and Eve were created in the image and likeness of God and they walked perfectly with Him. The environment God had provided for them was also perfect. God gave them a simple assignment: they were to be fruitful and fill the earth and exercise dominion over all the earth. Adam and Eve were destined to live forever. Sounds like a good life, doesn't it? According to Genesis 1:31, in God's eyes, everything was very good!

Now, God allowed Adam and Eve to eat of every tree in the Garden except the Tree of Knowledge of Good and Evil. God told them, *"in the day that you eat of it you shall surely die"* (Genesis 2:17). In this set-up, Satan quickly spotted a grand opportunity. He would go to Eve and convince her that God was purposely holding out on them. Satan would tell her that if she and Adam ate of the forbidden fruit, they would not die as God had said. In fact, he would tell Eve, God knew that in the day they ate of that tree, their eyes would be opened and they would be like God.

So Eve was confronted with a choice that day. Eve chose to eat of the forbidden tree. Then, she convinced Adam to eat of it also. By their acts of rebellion, sin came into the earth and came with a big price.

God Already Had a Plan

God is not surprised by anything we do. He knows everything before it happens. So in His loving and gracious manner, he had already devised a plan by which the death penalty of sin would be paid once and for all. And by this plan, perfect communion between God and man would also be restored.

> The wages of sin is death, but the gift of God is eternal life in Christ Jesus our Lord (Romans 6:23).

The plan then? His Son Jesus was the plan. Jesus, the perfect sacrifice, was the only One whose death could pay the penalty of sin in full for all of mankind. And over 2000 years ago, Jesus accomplished that for us. He took all of man's sins upon Himself. Jesus, the Savior of the world, suffered and died on the cross to pay the penalty for sin for the whole world.

After His death, Jesus was placed in the grave. The good news: Jesus did not remain in the grave. No, the Father raised Him up on the third day and Jesus now sits in Heaven with Him. Why is that significant? It is significant for many reasons but I will mention just one reason here. Because God raised Jesus out of the grave, all who believe can rest assured that they too will be resurrected from the grave and spend eternity with God. Now that's good news!

> So when this corruptible has put on incorruption, and this mortal has put on immortality, then shall be brought to pass the saying that is written: "Death is swallowed up in victory."
>
> "O Death, where is your sting?
> O Hades, where is your victory?"

(1 Corinthians 15:54-55).

What Must We Do to Be Saved?

In order to receive this life Jesus has made possible for us (salvation), first, we must believe the truth that Jesus died to save us. Then, we repent and receive forgiveness for the sinful manner we have lived our lives (Romans 3:23). That is to say, we turn away from the lifestyle of sin in which we walked, which was leading to death. Let us understand, we have all sinned. We must make a conscious decision to turn away from that life and choose to follow Christ.

Then, according to Romans 10:9-10, *"If you confess with your mouth the Lord Jesus and believe in your heart that God has raised Him from the dead, you will be saved."* This passage is letting us know we are not to keep private our decision to follow Christ, but we need to tell somebody. Along the same lines, baptism is also an important step that proclaims our new life in Christ (see Mark 16:16).

Now, at this point, Christian fellowship becomes very important—for encouragement, for prayer, for worship, and for the study of God's Word. All of these activities help our growth in the Lord.

Of course, much more can be said about salvation—some things I know; some things I may not know just yet. But let us look to God to lead us into all truth for He is well able to do it.

About the Author

LINDA LOUISE CLIFTON is a dedicated Christian and voracious reader and student of God's Word. Out of her growing love and commitment to the Lord Jesus and her enjoyment of His Word came this, her first book, *Thank God!* A teacher at heart, she is an inspiring and thought provoking Bible studies teacher and group discussion facilitator. She attended Howard University in Washington, DC, received her Bachelor's degree from East Carolina University in Greenville, NC, and attended Vintage Bible College and Seminary in Winston-Salem, NC. Linda is a freelance writer, blogger, and editor. She has a daughter, a married son, and three grandchildren. Cooking and interior design are among her many interests. A native of Jacksonville, NC, Linda currently lives in High Point. Please be sure to visit Linda's website and blog at www.lindalclifton.com.

Made in the USA
Columbia, SC
05 June 2019